IMAGES OF BEING
DIANE GUARNIERI

Stonegarden.net Publishing
http://www.stonegarden.net

Reading from a different angle.
California, USA

StoneGarden.net Publishing
3851 Cottonwood Dr.
Danville, CA   94506

First StoneGarden.net Publishing paperback printing:
September 2011

First StoneGarden.net Publishing electronic printing:
September 2011

Visit StoneGarden.net Publishing on the web at
http://www.stonegarden.net.

Cover art by Mary Guarnieri
Cover layout by Peter Joseph Swanson

In Memory of Alfred Lawrence Sahms

Dedicated to my daughter, Mary Christina Guarnieri,
& my mother, Nancy Claire Sahms

Acknowledgements

Some of the poems in this collection have been published at *Many Mountains Moving, Southern Ocean Review, Wilderness House Literary Review, Philadelphia Stories Magazine and Anthology, Mad Poets Review, Mid-West Cultural Council, Fox Chase Review, Autumn Sky Poetry, Limited Editions and Folio* among others.

Table of Contents

Preface

I am an urban poet: born, raised and still residing in Philadelphia, Pennsylvania. Throughout the decades, time and technology have changed the lives of people around me, the cityscape, and as progress would have it, I, too, have changed. Environment, family, and place have had an undeniable effect on who I was, who I am, and who I will continue to evolve into. External and internal values enhance or compromise our state of being.

I write from having lived through a time when car rides to the Jersey shore had no air conditioning; from Philadelphia's end days as a manufacturing city (condominiums replacing mills); from unprotected work places, where my father and his two older brothers walked concrete floors of textile mills, until each one of them died from emphysema; from my grandmother, Madeline's slow suffocating death from asbestosis (worked a job in a Roxborough mill manufacturing brake linings for locomotives); from an encyclopedia salesman, traveling door- to- door, peddling sets of encyclopedias and fairy tales; from loan sharks taking advantage of the uneducated and poor; from the closure and demise of a church, where three generations of women in my family were married; from family values where addictive drinking was enabled; and from changing values of women's roles and place in society.

Each life is made up of images: images that are uniquely our own and images that merge into the lives of others. We all are an image of our own being in the collective human experience defined as life.

Another Shirley Temple

A curvy path, down steep steps
that lead to a sidewalk.
"Don't step on the cracks."
I tug on his tattooed arm
my blue name never washing off.
His *Popeye the Sailor Man's* grin
animated eyes squint.

He turns a doorknob
opening to barroom
black as a jelly bean.
Neon letters glow orange, red.
"A Shirley Temple and a Ballantine."
"Like valentine?" I ask.
He winks.

One, two buckle my shoes
lift off of a sticky floor
and I sail to the top
of a red stool
bobbing like the cherry
in my sweet drink.

A jukebox weeps.
I spin round and round to a 45
to a voice blooming:
Red Roses for a Blue Lady
skip to *A Tisket, a Tasket*
find a dartboard, shuffleboard
but nobody plays here.

So I feed a nickel to a machine

and lifting a metal tongue
cashews slide down a chute
into my palm.

I watch him empty
glass after glass of beer
talking about work, work
in the mill all night, night
while I sleep weaving dreams.

Raising a little glass
he drinks down brown stuff
like the lemon and honey
he spoons down my throat
when I am sick, insists I wear
raw onions in each sock at bedtime
to pull the fever out of me
through my feet.

After another little glass of brown
poured from a bottle with roses on it
he downs another beer
without stopping, burping:
"Exxcuusse me."

I laugh.
Red-faced men with whiskers laugh.
Patting my back
he orders me
another Shirley Temple.

My glass sweats.
The ice cubes rattle.
I jump down

from my stool
lead him out of the dark
as if we were leaving the movies
my blue eyes sting tears
from too much burning light.

We turn the corner
past the red roses that he planted
up three steps
through the doors
and onto the sofa where he stops
flopping like Popeye
after Brutus knocks him out.

I reach for his hand.

Hunger

He arrived at the patched, screen door
wearing glazed, wingtip shoes
carrying a hard selling song
as he entered the room.

His fingers unfolded brochures
arranging them like place mats
atop a teetering table
next to Inky the cat.

Shameful shelves clung close to the wall
dressed in cans of corn, beans, peas.
He stared at hunger in their eyes
and chimed: *Books are the key!*

Knowledge to feed children: A – Z.
Order now! There's still time
for me to discount the fairy tales.
Smiles shined: she marked a line.

The priceless box arrived. Each book
intoxicating as wine
gold letters of the alphabet
embossed upon its spine.

Once Upon a Time, they'd only look
at black ink letters, groups of words
twenty-five fairy tales never
to be sung, never to be heard.

Left Behind, Somewhere in Time

Driving, I steer to a place that no longer exists
the way that it use to when I viewed the passing world
from the back seat of my family's Plymouth Valiant.

The roads and intersections are the same.
Time traveling into the future never stops for red lights.
Gone is the Sears Building
 (Adams Avenue and Roosevelt Boulevard)
an implosion a couple years back.

The land remains yielding another crop of merchants.
My mind travels in reverse, parks for a while
outside straight lines of time.

I see clearly through yesterday's windows
feel the warm cushioned interior of days once lived
drive away carrying bags of my past with me
so I can stop every now and then
look back over my shoulder
at landmarks left behind, somewhere in time.

Snowman

We giggle
as you dip the tip of a paintbrush
into canisters of colors
painting three white circles
a green top-hat, black dots for buttons
a tinge of cherry-red, swirly nose
lips brush upward, a frozen grin
and frosted blue eyes
see through both sides
of the storm window.

The snowman reads
mom's angry lips
Don't stop at the bar!
watches you walk straight to work.

Three squirming bodies dress
in hues of velvet blues, parading
to church where the Holy Family lives.

Onward Christian soldiers
march homeward
baby Jesus nesting in our hearts.

The snowman's eyes dripping blue
see you slipping and sliding in dark slush
under Bethlehem's Star
staggering up porch steps.

We watch the poinsettia
crash onto the floor
exposing roots watered in moonshine.

We watch Mom's lipstick smile
shatter into tiny clay pieces
soil spilling, dirtying our shoes
as we pass through Silent Night.

On Christmas day,
mom hoses your art away
melting the snowman liquid as milk
into the petrified garden.

Diane Guarnieri

Rest Stop

Empty beer cans roll around her flip-flops
as unfinished sips splash her small toes.

Sitting beside his little girl, sharing the back seat
he belches, *Hon – I gotta pee*

to his wife as she steers past signs of towns
blurring by her white Plymouth Valiant.

The family dog's head hangs out the window
lapping up flowing currents of air

his panting tongue, dripping with drool
flaps like a pink sail in the wind. Large paws

with razor-sharp nails bite the upholstery, sometimes
striking her thighs where her shorts don't reach.

His voice bursts from held in pain, *Hon - I gotta pee.*
Grandma, a passenger in the front seat

sits steaming beside an extra-large stockpot
hauled along to cook "Live Crabs" in.

She shouts, *Samsy, tie it in a damn knot.*
We can't keep stopping every twenty minutes.

The wife gives in, pulling onto a gravel lot.
He disappears behind the door of "Joe's Bar."

Grandma says, *He's just like your father.*
The wife pulls hard on the door's handle,

Skipper, come on. Let's go for a walk
yanking the dog's leashed neck.

A quick voice jumps out, *Can I come too?*
Joining hands, they walk toward weeds.

The dog lifts his leg. With the leash lassoed
around the fender, Skipper anchors on the ground.

Grandma drifts away as July's rising tide
of heat engulfs the Valiant. Doors wide open,

windows all rolled down, and legs sticking
to red vinyl, mother's *abracadabra*

turns car into boat. Squirmy giggles ripple
through calm waters. Mother deals seven cards

guiding the way through "Go Fish." A winning smile,
curved like a hook, baits her mother's stare

as she counts and shouts, *I have the most pairs.*
Losing with grace, the mother fans her sweat

beaded face with a fistful of cards evenly spaced
in her losing hand. He reappears, dealer's choice,

casting a long shadow, staggering toward them.
Fresh white foam from the beer's head sticks

to his mustache above his glassy grin. Grandma
wakes, rocks the boat, whitecaps swell as she yells,

Samsy, what took you so long? It's as hot as hell in this car.

Oh Ma...cool... down. This... is... my va-ca-sh...in.

They travel toward the sea. Mirages of water
dance on the highway in front of her eyes.

Smell of beer everywhere.

Bell Bottoms

Incense glows hot orange to ash
blue smoke rises, a snake uncoiling
jasmine perfumes the one-room store
as her fingers weed through tightly spaced rows
of hip, psychedelic clothes
pick a pair of fuchsia flowers
overgrown with power.

In a full-length mirror
she kisses the lips of her opposite
slides one foot then the other
into widest of widest flares.
Hanging ten on floorboards
she swings and sweeps and sways
to *Wipe Out* – crashing sounds rolling

down out of a sun-bleached radio
surfing a shelf. She grooves
to the cash register shaking
its silver like a tambourine.
Flip-flops clapping the soles of her feet
soles of her flip-flops tapping the street
like hands on bongos keeping the beat.

Sparrow

Frail

hidden under a fake feather coat
with thin, spindly legs
wearing a skull cap

she has been spotted   flying
to the post office and food stores
but stays mostly inside her cage

though every day, even when ice crystals
form like patches on city lawn
she perches in her narrow yard

chirping noisily to her friends
breaking bread
crumbs gently gliding
through the large empty spaces

between her grasp.

Mister

Clock hands turn the wrong way and you, Mister,
move back slowly through time. Memory opens
to a silhouette, your body touching narrow door jams
a back-lighted doorway, scent of Cuban cigar
and sweat announce your arrival

Mister,

my father's account written in your pages of debt
your fifteen pound bulging book strapped with thickest bands
wrapped in your arms. Custom leather soles worn down
from walking on the sides of them - squeak, grunt with each step

Mister,

deafening machines, the night-shift buzz still humming, Mister,
in my father's hearing, brown dust rattling his lungs
oil and grime trapped beneath non-manicured nails
his short life-lined palm reaches, welcomes
your hand into his home. Your rump-roast hand shakes it

Mister,

Judas dressed as Jesus sent to calm the storm
in debt's drowning waters, row us out of shark infested poverty.
Your tight lips part hope of a sea opening to the promise land
as my father's kneeling words politely pray
in his Manayunk vernacular for a low interest loan

Mister,

to fix the family's leaking toilet, a lopsided titanic, Mister,

that you see sinking through the cracked ice
of our kitchen ceiling. You hear his confession
know his job doesn't have a pension, Union,
just one day off for Christmas, a week's vacation

Mister,

your thick-worm fingers tap numbers, endless numbers
while a curling ribbon spews from the mouth
of your adding machine positioned near plaster-less
holes that my embarrassed father points at
where mice collapse through, hide and jump out
of the toaster scaring his three nursery rhyme daughters

Mister,

your anvil voice drops a 30 % interest rate, Mister,
with your complimentary smile and coupon book
onto my father's head, as I remember it
'cause I was there, remember

Mister.

Miss Thompson

Memory's haunt flies me to her porch, heavy oak door
where my eyes search beyond splintering steps
that could lead me away from this bolt releasing moment

Vanish! before the door swings open, yet
I see through misty window
time ticking sadness, pendulum swinging

My six year old body embraces poinsettia
entrusted to me by church elders
delivery of these bleeding petals

to my assigned "Shut-in," Miss Thompson.
Only knowledge of her
overheard gossip: *librarian type, old maid, childless.*

Musty smells embalm the air.
A cane.
A woman dressed in funeral.

Embroidered handkerchief dabbing her eyes.
Soles of orthopedic shoes scuffing... sliding...
Rolled down nylons encircling like soft anklets.

Hell...oo vibrating
over cracked lips, whistling teeth.
I watch myself walk cuddled flower

through a labyrinth of unhappiness.
No Christmas tree. No cookies.
Unplugged radio - silencing carols?

I hear myself lift *Merry Christmas,*
as if the presence of my words and poinsettia
could lighten her brick-stacked backpack

could summons a miracle to dimming eyes
to a mind on its own journey.
A radiator hisses, kitchen lights burn my eyes.

I look through time's window
and as an adult see
what I, the child, could not see

and seeing inside of seeing
a pregnant tear drop slides
the fragile pane of her face

her miscarried past.
No little angels.
Deafening silence of Christmas.

Chonce

This rattling window
mirrors
your phantom face

your shadowy image
preserved
in this chair

where you spent
the final chapters
of your life

lone as a monk
in clothes
you never changed out of.

You waited waited waited
in this chair
a passenger in Time's seat

holding a one way ticket to?
Where were you going?
Who was it you were waiting for, uncle?

Did you hear stampeding hooves
green horses crushing
hairs of the ground

a stage coach speeding
across a dehumanizing land
its driver

wearing no face
cape devoid of light
calling your name to his team?

Or did you wait for the ten turns
of seasons, the dropping of nature's
last leaf, a key,

to unlock
the lid of your coffin
buried body sinking?

It is here
here is where you grew roots
sitting in this wooden chair

this is your marker
this chair once a tree
this is the space

that marks your existence
more sacred than your headstone
chiseled with Charles, not Chonce.

Here inside this atmosphere
your spirit lifting, tug of time
inside your mystic mind

the shade is never drawn.

Still Life

Hung face
death watch white
eating through flesh

eyes shallow pools
of storm tossed blue
shadowing gray

eyelashes, eyebrows
hair and stubble: worried white
strays of forgotten brown

nostrils pinched by prongs
of tubing, his breathing machine
lips pale pink

ear canals flooded with
tick tock tick tock
circling minute hand
sentencing, menacing, tolling

arms, tired blue tattoos
one cancer lesion oozing
age spotted hands
dark freckle brown

wedding ring, gold
fingernails, splintering bone

beer belly ball
inflated under
fraying T-shirt, underwear

thinning yellow
traces of worn white

Dachau legs
flesh tones stretched
inflated ankles
soft surfacing skin

feet overlapping time
three years living
still life
breathing
dammed like a river

an invisible stake
driven through a man
pinned to a thin mattress
without a box spring
a wooden frame

His voice
fading   clear,
          This is Hell.

Easter

...the master of the house is risen up, and hath shut to the door... St.Luke 13:25

The old door swings open to find early spring.
Tender hearts bloom, *Alleluia* choirs sing.
Behind decaying walls, Whiskey is King.

Mom leads, *He has risen*, an off-key verse.
Children groom in Sears' finest Easter clothes.
The master of the house is inebriated, a sinful curse.

Hyacinths, lilies sweeten the cold air.
The wounds are revisited this time each year.
Memories still crouch low in fear.

The old door swings shut. The master is missing.
The hen gathers her brood under her wings.
Rejoice! Rejoice! Father has he risen?

Child of Dreams

Within my mind's tempestuous tides
where dream after hinged dream
opens door after door to

a child: streaming hair like sea anemones lifting
oyster-white face slow motion sinking
like one of Titanic's forgotten children.

I dive into depths of pool blue waters
swim into fear's nightmare
pull this drowning child to surface

and time after time, as I start CPR
my Trickster splashes cruel reality into my waking face
eyes focusing like a camera lens on objects inside my bedroom

and not knowing in seeing, not knowing in returning
not knowing in shadow of breaking light if this inner child wears
dead wings of a nightingale or rising wings of a lark?

A crestless wave softly sways
pushes me forward -
I press this child, a sea flower, between dry pages

until a hook pulls me under again
and I am Tiresias struggling
in murky waters unclear as a cedar lake

I grope for dangling limbs, seaweed hair
then I appear among green hills
without her as I hear children's laughter

I am naked
I am outside
Shower in sunlight

A Wiseman tells me the child is safe.
I see her on a baby swing, freed.
We wake.

Diane Guarnieri

Madeline

Madeline is suffocating.
The caves of her eyes search fading light for
something to cling to. She breathes
in unison, death-rattle chorus, with

black lungs of coal miners
brown lungs of factory workers
dying lungs of asbestos workers.

Her soul excavates itself
like a cicada tunneling out
shedding her chrysotile corpse
freeing iridescent wings for flight.

Daisy

She sings aluminum, sometimes tin
thinking of her hymnal mother:
a chain linking generations of cleaning ladies
all of whom scrubbed urinals, bathroom walls
where elementary school boys competed
to see whose stream could hit the target:
a raised radiator steaming.

Chalk dust, pollen yellow, lifts like incense
as she claps erasers, prays to her God
for her daughters' deliverance
from this, her daily bread
from this, her daily dance.

Keys jingle, encircling a ring
paper clipped to the elastic
waistband of her polyester pants
adorned by tiny lint balls
that cling close like soft hope.

Her demeanor stems
above her perennial labor:
auditorium pipes snowing asbestos
chemicals like pesticides seeping
into the petal of her skin.

Sun-filled face droops
stem of back curving, a cane,
white rays curl from exhaustion.

Last breath, release of seeds
caught in an updraft
all the leaves dancing.

Lily

cracked and chipped bone china
on the toilet seat of her sofa
forgetting her way to her bathroom.

They had to diaper her, a toddler
in an aged body heavy as marble.
Lily's hands fly swatters

hit images that only she could see.
Age: a gambler's wheel
spinning never stopping.

Address: random places
flying everywhere.
Telephone number: disconnected

inside her broken circuitry.
In therapy, her fingers
could not grip a zipper, maneuver a button

through the hole of a blouse, skirt;
her hands, once holy temples
pressed together in rosary prayer

broken pliers trying to clamp clothespins
to the perimeter of a wicker basket.
During meals, she'd bend and unbend the end

of a flexible straw using it to spoon soup
into her mouth. Her voice
a startled bell rang out:

Alle sind Nazispion!
Alle sind Nazispion!
Lily sat between metallic arms

of her wheelchair; an unknowing
darkness funneled into her eyes
glazed over with a killing frost.

Machines, Machines, Monstrous Machines

He punched the clock at eleven, again at seven
ticking hours in between were spent walking isles of
machines, machines, monstrous machines

spitting fiber into textile air, damaging lungs
already filled from a daily pack of Pall Mall.
Machines, machines, monstrous machines

days to weeks, weeks to months
months to years and years and years…
Machines, machines, monstrous machines
tending them, humming inside their thunderous voices.

It was audible, not thunderous:
an oxygen machine breathed with him
transparent wire tubing ran the floorboards
connecting tank to nostrils
a talking body on a long permanent leash
Machines, machines, monstrous machines

From living room bed to front door
walking, a burden for such a man
walking floors of the Textile mill, faded
walking sandy beaches of Jersey, faded
walking sidewalks of Manayunk faded
faded, faded … along with sounds of
machines, machines, monstrous machines

They brought him to this sterile room.
Respirator reaching its ugly arm
down deeply inside his chest.
Abused, poisoned, worn out
his machine beyond repair.

Nothing could save him, save him, save him
his life, laboring with, with, with
machines, machines, monstrous machines.

All up in smoke
Machines, machines, monstrous machines

Thunderous no more
Machines, machines, monstrous machines

Dark Art

Inside a skull's crystal ball
cataracts cloud eyes
as long gray strands
limply blow over shriveled breasts
like weeping willows
caressing earth's nakedness.

Wild whiskers grow from
raised moles like onion grass
cast-iron heart's boiling bubbles
cavernous mouth spews nonsensicalness
hisses from a black tongue
belaboring brewing spells

chants: *a ram's testicles like my husband's*
a lion's heart large as my son's
a scorpion, my daughter-in-law
drops of royal grandchildren's blood
as the long reach of her stirring, stirring spoon
casts darkness into her victims' unconsciousness.

Their hypnotizable eyes.

Crocus

you appeared white
as swaddling
with a veined stripe

until the storm's black cape
covered you
stoned you

your inner wicks ablaze
petals pressed in waxy prayer
stem, strong as a palm tree

and if I were you
I think I would have given up
as I believe you did

my mystery

and as the pendulum
swung the sun
back into calm

you crocus, an oasis
in a desert of snow
vertebrae broken

in spirit blowing wind
disappearing
as if you were never here

Baby's Breath

She opens the nursery door again

remembers
an upside-down bouquet
unfolding
beneath her heart-tied ribbon

remembers
life gently wrapped
inside a receiving blanket
small breaths
gentle rise and fall
of a newborn tide

remembers
a face   a barren moon
pressing her ear near
infant nostrils
pressing her breath
into unmoving lips   nose

remembers
madness   howling
a needle piercing time's eye
lullabies unsung
cradle   rocking emptiness

She closes the nursery door   again

Stitches
for Mary

Sheer white gown drapes over you
like a cut out on a paper doll.

Art in his doctoring needle
an expert tailor knots

black thread after sewing
eight miniature lines like railroad ties

under the soft plum of your chin.
I, the dish: you, the spoon

run away from Emergency.
At home you press "Play"

on the VCR singing small soprano -
I love you, you love me -

with a purple tyrannosaurus
we have re-named Barnard.

Sleep like diamonds sharply cuts
into your eyes, my dream catcher

arms net my little feather.

Broom

He has me squatting, again
in the corner of my mind.

My reflection in the beveled belly
of the stainless steel tea pot

screams out
that things are warped, again.

I hide a frightened mouse
cornered in a dark room.

He towers,
swinging his broom of words

scraping worn floorboards
stirring settled dirt

sweeping me up
into another dusty storm.

Tiger Lily

Around the bulb of my heart
he sings haloes, tells me to be
his orange ray of reaching sunshine
his tigress, his lily, his star petals.

My body's bloom pours
out of itself
has poured out of itself
for countless summers
each one I have faded more and more
have become a midnight lily
under erotic sweat and moonlit fantasies.

I bloom my last
close in reverent devotion
knowing
perennials are not eternal

nor is love.

Irises

The purple ones are in bloom
and she cuts them
brings their strength inside
they have survived
another winter
blooming their celebratory splendor
unforgotten by Our Lady in mourning
and she loves them more than ever
in miraculous May, month of Mary.

Iris, who bears the flower's name
prepares their Mother's Day meals
as her husband and children tease
It's only a Hallmark holiday.
She lets the screen door slam
in evening's haunting light
her scissors cutting more stalks
green as swords of leaves
purple as bruised Hail Marys.

Love-Lies-Bleeding

never fading
these tendrils hang heavy;
I have woven them
into a red shawl
that drapes my heart
as it beats to the drum
of the drinkers' disease

never fading
father vomiting
my parents fighting
as their parents fought
battles reenacted

never fading
barroom jesters' stumbling dance
fools who lived inside my family tree
roots in darkness
cannot live light

never fading
this life sentence
long after corrupted deaths
roots I have inherited
run through my body
into bloody stems
leaves' reddish glow

never fading
my leaf–like tongue flapping
in the dark storm warning
you, since you were old enough to listen

never fading
autumn's new bowed bleeding

a knife cuts, reopens thick scars
a concealed flask inside your jacket
bottles hidden inside dresser drawers

never fading
web I am caught in again
this toxic blood
oh, my son

White Chrysanthemums

I plant autumn mums
inside a wooden crate
remember her:
hair wild as a blizzard
lima bean eyes
onionskin thin as fading petals.

Frost extinguishes life
smothering, cold
stiff as December mums
twigs brittle- browns.

Silhouettes against sunset
copper coin sun slowly dropping
into a slit in the horizon
rectangular box nesting death.

Chinese White Pine

By the sea,

your heavy trunk leans forward
in July's white heat

planted here, in time
you would step out of yourself

out of this brick-lined wall
(a homemade planter's box)

walk straight across sky
toward home

if only rooted chains
were not keeping you here

where season after season
you bear seeds, give shade,

offer fallen needles
to soften the ground.

Evergreen branches
lift endless prayers

like Tibetan monks
chained to their mountain

for the same reasons.

Fallen

She tucks clothespins
inside her apron pocket, folds
all the tattered and the torn, loops
the clothesline: thumb, elbow and slides
callused feet up concrete steps.

She carries her sunset within her.
Her mind, a broken basket.

He parks his work truck
turning the engine off, places
keys inside his empty chest pocket;
through the barren yard, past
rusty poles battered boots stir dust.

He walks twilight.
Leaf scar thoughts.

Together, they dine alone.
Cannibals, each of the other's heart.

Persephone Escapes Hades

Looking to the answers
climbing outside this fortress
away from the one

whose darkness fed on her
smothered the window-light
of her eyes.

She is no longer
ball and chained
to the kitchen's inferno

to his voice, a scorching echo
to his fire-flaming tongue:
bitch, dope, dumb

cunt, whore, bi-polar
witch, schizophrenic
lesbian, man hater.

Her words
keys unlocking doubt.
Unfettering hands.

Hidden spring of her inspiration
conversations with flowers.
On and off the page her voice singing

her mind's feet dancing with poets
strength of Chorus;
with Apollo's risings

through musing, through dreams
she did not starve into blind death -
rides Pegasus bareback

leaves this her tragic myth.

Mimosa

Just this tolling day
rooted in May -
Mimosa you are dead!
He always hated you
could never sing through
your fluted branches
blossom pink-whisker flowers
or dance segmented leaves
of summer's emeralds.
Marriage silenced in shadow.
Haunting: unloved skeleton
like coral outside of the sea
leafless branches
scratch the face of the wind.
No rustle of music left to sing.

Bleeding heart

Outer petal of heart's flower
splits like a separation
sheds its last drop of hope
white as a frosted teardrop.

Night and day
this heart hangs
on the arched stem of marriage
fading, thin as crepe paper

until it divorces itself
from the bond
that it once thrived upon

falls onto blades
severed into two equal parts.

Morning Glory Blues

Morning Glory Blue

her woven blanket - warmed her body, night and day
                withering years, her bed-ridden life

sanctuary - at the close of each petal day

sail - blowing the boat of her bed
        into undercurrents of her soul's deep pulling

chrysalis - sleep within butterfly wings of dreaming

        ***

Morning Glory Blue

became her shroud - image pressed into each fibrous pore

an uprooted blanket - he pulled it from her empty mattress

a cape – vine strangling heaviness encircled his shoulders
        until he folded floral memories into each soft crease

        ***

Morning Glory Blue

a garden - spread onto his bed, roots burrowing

at night - a curtain closes
        he sees her on a stage of dreams
        where reality is weightless as shadows on the moon

        ***
Morning Glory Blues bloom over his island of loss.

Le Pont Japonais a Giverny

Permanence of colors:
a bridge, lily pond
long-haired willows
like maidens weeping. Our
lives, lotus blooms, opened
toward each other and
in your absence our minds speak
in visions, poetry and dreams
silent as still water
beneath the bridge
that connects us -
you from one side
me from the other.
I see you, feel you
roots burrowing
into murky soil of
heart's hidden sufferings.

Nocturne

you meet me
in the darkness of indecision
without pathways

you tell me
follow the spinning sun
even as comets plunge into planets
asteroids smash into dust

you pull me
toward your galaxy
guide my eyes to see star patterns
to understand
that what we allow to possess us
is lifeless as our moon

The Kiss
after Gustav Klimt

Ivy halos his hair.
Draped over her ankles
vines dangle like willow leaves
there is immortality here
entwined outwardly - inwardly

White as moonlight on limbs
she is kneeling-death beside him
corpse face, eyelids closed
wears a shoulder-less robe
with tangent circles, some red as poppies,
no beginnings - no endings

Coal-curly hair. He is centered.
Face, a hidden sunrise
rectangles on his heavy robe
strength upon pillar of strength
black – white: absence - presence

Below their waists: circles - rectangles
merge, patterns intermingling,
as if his rectangles were doors
her circles - knobs
shapes fitting together, into each other
harmonious as sun, moon

One of his hands supports her cheek
the other like a weathervane points
to the temple of her wisdom, where
embedded flowers encircle her thoughts
as his lips, light as fallen leaves,
press against her snow covered cheek
they have entered each other: they are air

Release

Flamingo pink
scarlet
lavender
woven through gold
dance the horizon alive
 and I am
given grace
of another sunrise
his blue-sun eyes
melted the ice sculpture
freed a pink butterfly within
wings spread open lifting
freed the caged woman
set sail the ship in the bottle
unlocked my rusted heart
after volcanic years
by shining
rising
breathing breath
into my dying being

Free as a Dream

we are each other
you and I
unbound, unafraid
wiser than Icarus
immortal as Pegasus
rising across purplish-blue
only our shadows falling

we choose what it is
we want to remember
of the hard-ground past
before we were able to fly
high above the spinning
in order to forget
our wings lifting

Forest for the Forgotten

1.
if it had to occur, why
did it hit me broadside?
I walk.
My mind is somewhere
in a forest
I have lived inside
my entire life

2.
you found me
wondered how a wild flower
could go unnoticed
how it had enough light
to grow
surrounded by choking weeds
shaded by angry trees

3.
perhaps my dreams
will unriddle truth

My foot in a white
flip-flop
a gnarled tree root
chained my ankle
to the forest floor

then another ~

I was with you
then left you

my feet bare
I found my shoes

4.
When I awoke
there was snow
all over the house.

I left footprints
took a shower
washing this week

off of my body
gathering wisdom
apple-by-apple

5.
I want to be awake.
Will I owe you?
You who have found love
songs to sing to me

6.
For you:

I cup my hands
around your heart
as if I was holding
a monarch

every corny love song
closes my mind's doors
 from subway stop
to subway stop

I'm seated inside
thoughts of you

my inner thighs and lips
warmed by simmering desire
 at any given moment
I could drink all of you
inside of me

Images of Being

She, Duchamp's nude
descends onto his canvas
he brushes kisses/repetitive butterfly wings
Warhol silk screens onto her flesh

this act of mind
brush of tongue
slides the curved ridge of spine
Cezanne's seasonal study

Picasso fingers/brushes/soft piano hammers
strike inner strings
until warmth bursts forth
tasting yet not tasting/drinking yet not drinking
her into himself

this wilderness of unknowingness/Daliesque
consciously/unconsciously
his art/her dreamscape image
bodies' arousal/touching colors

so when he leaves
darkened studio
she feels flutter/each monarch moment
taking flight

Absence of Blue
for Johnny

Do the roots stop growing when a tree
is chain sawed to the ground? She digs up part
of the past, cradles some roots gently in her hands
their dangling fibers like fine baby hairs. Memory
of seed a mother carries within is always there. Some
roots cannot be destroyed in heart's soil.

From the mantel, she took the last happy, frozen-
faced moment of him down. Framed
by misfortune, she cut out his missing-in-action eyes
held them, paper seeds, in the lifelines of her palm
watered them with tears.

Now, his photo has two holes: absence of blues
absence of childhood and adolescent truth clouded out
by filler paper she places like a white sheet behind his head.
He cannot be replaced. The spaces that once were his eyes
have no feelings. His stare, bleached as November's sky
a white-washed wall, no recollection of blue.

Drowned Faces

lay in a mass grave
long boat of a box
none of them moving.

She touches them
with the care that one takes
when lifting someone
who is sick with too much hurt

arranges them in a vase
filled with tap water
she has mistaken for tears.

Each of the twelve buds
a bruised brain
burgundy, purple pain

each hanging head
layered inside itself
wears a crown of shame

each seaweed leaf- arm drooping
each battered body-stem aching.

From across the room
they could not, would not
sing bloom

for the two-faced hand
that signed the card:
with lies of love, lies, lies, lies

they whispered in corpse chorus
antiqued with agony
they remained bloomless

their listless faces, beautiful
in light of unsung truth.

Haunt

fist stuck there on the taped glass of a tiffany light

broken spines, decapitated legs of caned-back chairs

basement weeping, tears streaming, rising puddle in floor's depression

swearwords breathe beneath paint

bruised and splintered floorboards creak

flight of running footsteps imprinted on staircase

walls cradle hysterical echoes

woodwork around busted lock, pockmarks of scarred screams

hairline fractures slither through walls

thunderous slamming of doors, doors, doors

ghost of a murdered dining room table troubles the room

long length mirror reflects a shoved body, almost

breaking: penetrating the reverse world of light

Roller Coaster

Confined to a world of small spaces, size of a coaster's car, my body belted,
fastened by an extra bar, chain rattling jolt, long haul up, incline of years,
                                        picking up speed around
turning seasons, stomach punch
                        drop, fast and furious downward plunge
                                hair flung upward
nerves exploding, regrouping
                smaller inclines
                        declines, and then again,

chain rattling jolt, long haul up…

Could never exit.

Then the blistered, peeling paint, warping wood, crisscross web of planks
wobbly as tired legs. Twenty-three years violent as thunderstorms.
Hard hits against unpadded surfaces. Bruises. Brain banged around.

I escaped.

Fortune teller reads prominent peaks and valleys; tells me a palm never lies.
My dream:

> *I am riding in the final car and after each hill and turn*
> *it jumps the track. The last hill, the hitch breaks.*
> *Free from the car, I fall (*slow motion)
> *collapse on concrete.*

You released yourself, she whispers. I weep.

Geisha

She descends.
Kimono sleeves like Japanese fans
fold in upon her
resting inside solitude
her heart, a heavy paper weight.

She listens
to the soulful wind, as strength lifts
from mountain mist, frozen joy
melts into mirrored waters'
rippling reflections.

She returns
changed, yet unchanged
embraces all she thought she lost
heart lifting a wingspan
of self-forgiveness.

Crow & Dove
after Lamentation by B. Reisman

Framed in black and white unable to speak
a man holds a dead crow in upturned palms, but
this is not about the dead crow
this is not about the ominous flock of recurring crows

nesting in leafy camouflage high above bedroom windows
or crow crackling noises (spinning hypnotic sounds)
like witchy spells from wing of dusk to break of sky.

This is not about fledglings that fell
from womb of nest to their death.
Crows are not responsible for this.

A man's mind lures him to be evil
portrayed through:
dark weepy eyes of a fish trapped in a net

eyes like marbles rolling around the skull's sockets
eyes strapped in the straitjacket of loneliness
eyes housed inside their own asylum
eyes not able to see

how she is running, running, running
down a narrow street   her back to his back
hands releasing her hidden dove

naked arms flung upward
in freedom's flight like praise
into beginning: into new life

without him

Everyone Has Their Own Story

1. Thursday, October 18th

you are my friend
and I sing you free of this sin
you poisoning your mind, body
didn't you learn, didn't you know
that you are beautiful

you read Dorothy Parker's
"you might as well live"
and Anne Sexton's
Live or Die

my poetic sister
there are no words for this
you opened Pandora's box
taking all those pills
I have no place in this poem
nor words for you, no words

why did you love
Sylvia's death poetry so much?
as if she was pulling you
from the other side
as if she wrote them to you

I'm afraid

you may not be Lady Lazarus
you may not come back
and be yourself

I pray Atropos,
Don't cut the thread of
my friend, my friend, my friend

2. Saturday, Oct. 20th

the sky yesterday was dark over your home
slate clouds moved swiftly
a hawk circled only once

the red brick road I drove over
countless times dropping you off
at your front porch steps

awaits your footsteps
the church steeple across from your house
is lonely as van Gogh's in *Starry Night*

I have spoken to Harry and Ellen
everyone reacts differently to the news
everyone has their own story

each filament of the web
is woven around you
and you lie at the center
both prey and predator

today, I miss you again
this is the first day I haven't cried
I have told you countless times

to live ~live
only if you come back
not as lady Frankenstein.

3. Oct 29th, Monday

You didn't remember
it was my birthday;
I didn't care.

On your birthday,

you laughed when I opened
the trunk of my car:
a dozen helium balloons
popped out quickly as a Jack in the Box.

We jumped up and down
laughing, bouncing
children of the night.

It was Saturday the last time we spoke.
You, wanting to escape from the hospital
like a jailbreak, hung up on me
when I would not help.

Today, you signed yourself out.
Called and told me you were walking home
in pajamas. I didn't ask if you had a coat.
It was too late for that.

You said you were going to another place
to get the help you needed.
Two dollars to get you home, pack things
especially books.

I wanted to tell you not to take Sexton/Plath
but I could not.

Your voice is not the same.
The medical team plunged something
down your throat
to help you breath, to keep you alive
when you choked on your own vomit.

You joked, said you were Tinkerbell.
We laughed.
You said you were tired of crying.
You said I am always there for you.

I don't want to be anymore.
I cannot bring my voice
which has remained the same
to be wicked
to tell you the ugly truth
that you need to go on without me.
I don't want to be your friend anymore.

I still want to protect you.
My umbrella, a shield,
is full of bullet holes.

Dark clouds surround you
will always surround you
I know you are tired of being sick.

I am tired of being rained on.

Your Tinkerbell voice flew away
you, who became Dorothy
somehow, found your Wizard.
A balloon voice is trapped
in the subway and
there is no Glinda there.
I cannot be her. This time
the Wizard will guide his balloon
to your home.

You say you will sign yourself in.
A birthday present for me
I think?
Yet you call again
wheezing as you run, run, run
and
about being chased
they, they, they want to 302 me
You keep telling me
Rasping static…

You had to go ...

4. Mischief Night Day, October 30th

I cut a frown
into the Jack-O-Lantern's face
wanting to know
how you are.

Not in the hospital
not committed
doing it your own way.

Upset that people know
of your coma, disease
your attempt to end your life.

The moon and sun
a duet singing mischief
light and darkness
endless risings, settings - shades of blues.

5. November 1 - All Saints Day

who among us are saints?
it's hard to say
I believe this day
only in the survival of self

shut-in from the cold
you say for three months
like the clover
St. Patrick's trinity

pneumonia, your nemesis
rides the breeze
a surfer in a wet suit

ready to reside within you

fluttering Tinker bell wings
of your voice tell me
you're unable to see the doctors
going outside is death

and my metamorphosis
into forty-eight has
turned a key inside
a rusty lock, my heart

opens a red rose
inside my thorny self
in this new found autumn day
unafraid to walk

as saint, as sinner

Narcissus

I, Narcissus, pine for my past.
Daphne of a different genus.
Memories of a human act.

In Ovid's *Metamorphoses*, I was cast
the young, handsome Narcissus.
I, Narcissus, pine for my past.

I, a bloom of a man, to enchant.
My interest: hunting (not male or female asses).
Memories of a human act.

Why must I love another? I'd ask.
I, Narcissus, bewitched into loving my own kiss.
I, Narcissus, pine for my past.

Unrequited love wore my death mask
my shadow reflected in dark waters of Styx.
Memories of a human act.

Greek and Roman Mythology outlast
me, me, Narcissus,
I, Narcissus, pine for my past.
Memories of a human act.

Aubade
for Joe

During your absence (these last two and a half years)
every one of us a prisoner: kept from each other, yet

within the dominion of recurring dreams, you appear
always a small child who finds his way home to me

where surreal peace exists
no waking barricade: no hidden grievances

where a mother's heart is consoled -
no pain, no need to weep.

Outside my bedroom, on the edge of the eaves
my prayers waver, sink with dying darkness

embed into every disappearing dream
wait for the rising of your return.

Snow Covered Rhododendron

Yesterday, there was only one sparrow.

Today - two.

They are more grayish then brown,

coal-speck eyes not much larger than sesame seeds.

One darted its beak (two times) into the lingering snow.

Drinking it? Perhaps.

Disappointment met my eyes when they left the cold

bush like an abandoned home. My thoughts rest inside this poem.

My eyes see only an empty place where minutes ago they perched.

Why do I have the need to share this with you?

Maybe, there is a metaphor here or

maybe, I just wanted you to know.

My Lover

Whose hair is swan white wisdom
Whose thoughts are a camera lens focusing
Whose eyebrows are slivers of moon silver glow
Whose eyelashes are fringes on black shoe laces
Whose eyelashes are grasshoppers' antennae
Whose ears are shells listening to everyone's roaring sea

My lover

Whose nose is a sun dial
Whose nostrils are black helium balloons
Whose mouth spins delicate silken strands
Whose lips are firefly wings
Whose teeth are strings of stolen pearls
Whose tongue is rhythm and blues

My lover

Whose chin is a carp sunning in upper waters
Whose neck is a steel beam
Whose throat smolders ashes of bourbon, chasers of beer
Whose chest is Mt. Everest
Whose shoulders are Simon's forced to carry other people's crosses
Whose one arm is Jacob's ladder, the other a tire-jack

My lover

Whose wrists are nightsticks
Whose fingers are hinges and levers pulling triggers
Whose grip is a Venus fly trap
Whose irises are blue hurricane lamps
Whose soul is a forsythia blossom burning brightly with renewal
Who is the vast-wide openness of freedom

My lover

With a back broader than an ironing board
With thighs powerful as a jack hammers pounding
With the tease of a million open-tailed peacocks' eyes
With legs the arc of triumph
With feet of a dog's scratched back

My lover

My lover with eyes of a savage pirate
My lover with eyes of blue-jay wings
My lover with eyes that are tail lights of trains trailing along tracks
My lover with eyes that are unexplored holes in the ocean floor
My lover with eyes that are the Milky Way's sparkling
My lover with eyes eternal

My lover

Diane Guarnieri

Footprints

I felt them
your footprints leaving
through my body's hallway

holy as a soul leaving its body
and inside absence of you
I hear the moment when

an owl's voice leaves
its hollow breast
entering air as question

who are you? You
whose presence fills emptiness
within me like baptismal water

and if I were an oak leaf
you would be the veins
running their pattern through me

Visit
StoneGarden.net Publishing Online!
You can find us at: www.stonegarden.net.

News and Upcoming Titles
New titles and reader favorites are featured each month, along with information on our upcoming titles.

Author Info
Author bios, blogs and links to their personal websites.

Contests and Other Fun Stuff
A forum to keep in touch with your favorite authors, autographed copies and more!

CPSIA information can be obtained at www.ICGtesting.com
Printed in the USA
BVOW022019161011

273728BV00001B/20/P